I0203165

Mirrors of Faith

Phyllis A. Comeaux

Mirrors of Faith
By
Phyllis Comeaux

Pebbles to Gold Publishing Company
ISBN: 979-8-9857039-6-2

Printed by Lulu

DEDICATION

This book of poems is dedicated with much love to all my children, Michelle, David, and Julie; their spouses, Jon, Desiree and Trevor; and all my grandchildren, Lily and Zoë, Autumn and Natalie, and Emmitt, Meyer and baby Palmer, as they learn to love and grow in love with the Holy Trinity through their own journey during quiet prayer time. The journey can be quite exhilarating if you can quiet your soul, wait and listen. And to my husband, John, who continues to live the journey with me, encourage me, gently admonish me along the way and patiently watch as it unfolds.

I would also like to dedicate this book to my dear friend Jerry Barousse, who lost his wife this year, and who has been another beautiful example of love for Jesus and Mary and his deep Catholic faith. I will always remember the time he invited me to a praise and worship event at St Pius X. I had never met anyone so filled with the Spirit in praise and song as we waved arms and sang loud with spiritual energy that was so exhilarating. I pray for Shannon and the repose of her soul and for Jerry in his loss and sadness, though I know he finds comfort in the Spirit and in the church and his involvement in so many church activities and with the Knights and ACTS. He and Shannon did not have an easy life, but they always had incredible strength and faith through all the ups and downs, and they always had a good disposition, greeting all with a smile in spite of whatever challenge they faced—a perfect example of Christian attitude not only in the best of times, but also in the wake of trials and misfortunes.

Table of Contents

Phyllis Comeaux

INTRODUCTION

For those who have read my first volume of poems, "Portraits of Grace", you will recognize that the Holy Spirit has continued to bless me during prayer, adoration and meditation with inspirations and images for the next volume of poems that has come together in the last 10 months. Almost never do I sit down specifically to write a poem, except the ones for the family, which are not difficult since I have a very entertaining and colorful family whom I love so very much and seem to appreciate the poems I write for them. Since I now have 7 grandchildren, with 5 of them ages 5 and under who also live nearby, time is at a premium. So I sometimes will start a poem after prayer, then will have to finish it later. But thankfully, the Holy Spirit is quite understanding and I don't have to return to a deep state of prayer to be able to finish the poem. I can sit at the computer to type in what I have written and He must sit on my shoulder prompting the rest, as it fairly flows out without much rewrite.

The title "Mirror of Faith" has been an image that I have held onto since we did our Bible Study on James in 2013 and it resurfaces quite often as I contemplate where I am, how do I perceive my progress in Faith, Love and Charity and what does God actually see in me. Is my image accurate or quite distorted – only the Spirit knows that answer and I think the image wavers like a handheld mirror in a shaky hand, as I am sure my journey is in the right direction but has taken turns and missteps- hopefully fewer and fewer along the way. That is why it's important to me to look into the mirror and ask God what does He see and am I actually on the right path. I treasure my prayer time to get a sense of His response and try so hard to "listen" and see the "image in the mirror" so I may follow in the right direction—never sure if I am quite "getting it right", but always praying for a "tap on the shoulder" or being "tripped on the path," if I'm not.

I know that He does love me and always smiles on me, even when I'm not getting it quite right. He is so patient and forgiving, the kind of parent and grandparent I try to be. And so filled with love, always in spite of my shortcomings—the kind of spouse and friend I also try and want to be. So I hope you contemplate and enjoy looking into my Mirror with me and discover all the nuances that make up my journey and my relationship with my God and all of His creation.

Phyllis Comeaux

Mirrors of Faith

SPECIAL GLASSES

Wash away the tension
Tune out the discord
Smooth the ruffled feathers
Send the Holy Spirit
To take me away to a place
Where there is such Peace
That surpasses all understanding
As I stand in the midst of an avalanche
Waiting to be mangled by the crash

And suddenly I have not a care
As I am floating on air
How did I get here
While still sitting in my chair
My eyes see only beauty
As through special glasses
The eyes of the Holy Spirit
Have given me the vision
That makes life worth living
The frown that's on my face
Suddenly turns upside down

And my eyes are opened wide
To view the splendor all around
With vibrant color and dazzling sights
That evoke joy, peace and love
Flowers in colors I've never seen
Trees and plants incredibly green

Mirrors of Faith

Angels and saints with dazzling auras
Drifting among the beautiful flora
Flowing streams and babbling brooks
Entice me to desire more than a look

Beckoning me from Heaven above
To aspire to reach for this lofty goal
That many are called to behold
But few persevere or even hear
The sound of the call in their soul
Or like me, feeling distressed
At the looming boulders about to fall
Not aware this may be a test
Of Faith and trust, no need to stress
Stay calm and without fear
Just wait for the vision to become clear.

And behold through my special glasses
I see these boulders big and tall
Are really stones of little stature
And looking closer, I'm amazed to see
They're unpolished gems waiting for me
To expose all of their true beauty
Gifts you've given me to unwrap
Whose value is seen when the time is right
Through special glasses that improve my sight
To reveal the gift in Your true light

May 21, 2023

CONQUERING MY SOUL

Please, Lord, I beg of thee
Do not let me be conquered
By another on this very day
As I seek Your protection
From the evil around me
For this, I fervently pray

Fill me with abundant joy
In place of this distress
So I am not annoyed
By what seems such a mess
As my plans become void
And suddenly useless

Take me out of the wasteland
That I find myself deep in
As I am parched and dry
There is no place of comfort
And I begin to cry
Yearning to leave this desert
        Day is Done

With great determination
That I must undertake this quest
I decide to fight the evil that lurks
To destroy the peace, disturb my rest
Clothed with the armor of God

I am ready to be put to the test

Anger and bitterness squelched by my torch
Discouragement slashed by my sword
Sadness is lassoed and bound tight
Dismay is pierced with a lance
My angels are with me as we fight
    Battle won through the Night

    New Day Begins
Hope springs up, uncovering a well
Flowing waters that soothe my soul
Bathing me in Your good graces
Washing away the gritty sand
You lift me out of the crystal water
Fresh and clean I take Your hand

Now I have found a place to rest
Having survived another test
I let out a sigh as peace flows in
Ready for the new day to begin
Looking forward to the joy to come
As we have conquered the evil one
You have conquered my soul

May 25, 2023

THE LANGUAGE OF LOVE

How do I communicate
With the One that I dearly love
How do I kiss Him or give Him a hug
When He resides in Heaven above
The answer comes over some time
Brought to me on the wings of a dove
Dropped on me in our special place
Where we daily meet to share our love

Nestled in my chair where I always pray
I ponder on the Words that touch my heart
While reading the scriptures of the day
I treasure the love notes that come to me
As I discern what He has to say
My heart begins to feel the depth of love
That permeates me in a special way
Fills my soul to overflowing where it may

Rising to go about my daily tasks
I feel a nudge to take some action
What is it, as I ponder and ask
And I receive a love note to pass on
To someone who needs a word of cheer
As they are feeling lost and alone
So I call to share the love of Him
That goes through me to this special someone
Fulfilling His wish; giving them a lift

Love notes come throughout the day
The urge to share a hug or give a kiss
To stop and pray for those in need
To do a task in loving service
To humble myself, drop to my knees
It's not about me, but those You wish
To know the love of the Lord through me
Then I get the final love note that is Mine
Day well done my lovely one, a kiss goodnight
Fills me with His peace and Love divine

June 13, 2023

STAINED GLASS

A beautiful white dove
With wings spread in flight
Suspended in the window above
Rays of glory and bright light
Emanate outward from the alcove
Much to my sheer delight
Seeming to reach out to my pew
As I enjoy the breathtaking view

Then the dove comes to life in a flash
And soars crashing through the stained glass
Flying through the rafters of the church
As it seems to be searching for a perch
Or an open heart in which to enter
And settle to redeem the wayward sinner
Left and right, up and down
He continues to circle all around

This Spirit of Life has its target
Coming straight to the heart of my soul
Crashing through the fragile glass
That surrounds my delicate heart
Now stained, dirty and droll
Intent on mending the broken shards
And restoring the beauty within
He searches for the weakest part
To fortify it to persevere to the end

He spreads His wings with determination
To revive the original creation
With colors vibrant and bold
Drawing toward it, He circles around
And enters, though I am hardly aware
Until I feel the growing within
Soon I think my heart will burst
As it's filled with love and joy
And when it does the colors that show
Reflect that beautiful stained-glass window

June 13, 2023

THE LOOKING GLASS

When I gaze into the looking glass
What do I find?
Is it a reflection of myself
Or thy love divine
Do I see a hardened face
Or one that's soft and kind
One frowning at every interruption
Or smiling through the pain
I hope to see the love You sow
And then to look and watch it grow

And as I look once again
Do I see the shoulders broad and wide
For the things that I have done with pride
As well as those I choose to hide
Covering the blemishes that are inside
But maybe the shoulders are rounded in humility
Head down, eyes to the ground
Asking for pardon and peace
Assuming nothing, emptying self
To receive the grace You have for me
This is what I hope to see

We are born in the image of God
That should reflect in the glass all of our days
But often it fades, we forget who we are
Letting the world shape our image and ways

Instead of beauty, radiance and love displayed
We look weathered, battered, hardened or crazed
Nothing there to share with others
Empty look, empty heart doesn't bother
In this barren, deserted lonely place

But keep looking my child, continue to gaze
You will find the true image through the haze
The one that reflects God and all of His ways
Keep seeking and find it day after day
That reflection will become who you truly are
You have absorbed the light like the mirror
A vision of tenderness, compassion and love
That emanates through you from Heaven above
Not a magical mirror, but a funnel of love
Through the Looking Glass

June 15, 2023

HOLY SENSUALITY

My Jesus
My senses are heightened
Every time I am in your presence
My day becomes brightened
And I am filled with Your essence
Feeling as though I am glowing
Surrounded by Your effervescence
The feeling keeps growing
So I remain in your presence

Even behind closed lids
I can see You with the eyes of my mind
Your crystal blue eyes and gentle smile
Would draw me near even if I were blind
As they beckon me to come to Your side
And my heart skips a beat at the thought
Of us both in a comfortable embrace
Filled with love and pouring out grace

Ears of my heart
Hear the whispers of Your Word
Barely audible, I take the hint
Handling it carefully like a sword
What is the message You have meant
For me to discern as Your poignant Word
That pierces my heart and has me repent
Or fills me with joy that is so intense
I am startled by the effect on my senses

Touch of Your Spirit
Brushes ever so softly upon my soul
And I feel the tingling from head to toe
'Til soon I am certain I must have a glow
As it spreads through my being with so much warmth
It's coming through my pores for all to see
I wonder if they know what has happened to me
The love of my Jesus is so immense
I am certain they perceive the secret I hold
His love for me is so blatant and bold

Taste of You
The wonderful part that is most intimate
More than a passionate kiss upon the lips
You give to me all of yourself
In the most wonderful sacrifice of all
That I may take You into my body
To taste on my tongue and then become one
As I return to my pew, savoring all of you
Wanting that moment never to end
But knowing that soon it can happen again
A sensual love, your gift to me

June 22, 2023

Phyllis Comeaux

THE BELL RINGS FOR ME

I was but a young wayward "child"
When we started this journey together
Though 50 years of my life had passed
I knew we'd be together forever
You had played with me in my early years
And I was delighted is so many ways
But the journey began with the sound of a bell
And I knew your Spirit was at hand

It's time to grow up, to do some work
Was the message that came my way
 A vision of me, a child in a field
Working with the Father every day
He planted seeds to increase the yield
While I watered, weeded and prayed
Then together we'd rest side by side
Or I'd run through the fields and play

Sometimes there would be fences to mend
Thorny brambles to dig up from the ground
Or youngsters and newborns to tend
And we would gather them all around
Feeding and nurturing 'til day's end
Never a moment did I have a frown
I loved being with my Father, my friend
Taking part in the fruits that abound

And you smile and whisper "Go on, run and play"
And I romp through the fields of golden grain
With my hair blowing back in the wind
Free as a bird flying, swooping, up and all around
Loving these unique moments we share
And I return to You and settle myself down
As You let me know how much You care
For me and all of Your creation

The time will come when I hear the bell again
That the day is nearly over
You send your Spirit to call me home
And I will be with You forever

July 8, 2023

THE NARROW PATH

As I pray that my sins are forgiven
By the One who wears the crown
And gave His life for you and me
That we could all be heaven bound
And live with Him for eternity
Down the road ahead I can see
A glimpse of what waits for me
Narrowing to a point of impossibility
The eye of the needle

I pray the Spirit to help me
To make the choices that will be
The path that's straight and narrow
Hitting the bullseye like an arrow
I can see the gate at the end of the road
Seems so small from this far away
How will I get through I wonder and pray
I must focus and try not to stray
I cannot miss the mark

Others are meandering on adjacent paths
Heading in the general direction
But distracted by many sounds and sights
Wandering after butterflies and flowers
Or curious and interesting formations
Things of this world have beauty indeed
But may hinder the journey if we do not heed
The warning that we must enter the narrow gate
If getting to Heaven will be our Eternal fate

Others are with me on the narrow path
Whom we help and encourage along the way
We talk and share, care and pray
And some do stumble and fall
Needing to be carried a bit
But we know whom to call
He's walking alongside us already
Jesus, our companion is steady

Sometimes the path is very rocky
Or overgrown with thorns and thistles
Nary a stream to take a drink
Nor fruit or bread to stop and eat
Yet none complain of hunger or thirst
As the end of the road comes first
The servant Jesus leading the way
And the dove behind us every day
Somehow satisfies our every need
What a miracle indeed

The end of the road, a very narrow door
No human can make it through
But one by one, as He calls our name
Suddenly we're in the beautiful garden
Preparing for the Wedding Feast of the Lamb
Shed your clothes and don your gown
Dazzling white with brilliant gems
You are about to be presented to Him
The Bride of Christ waiting no longer
To see His face in this heavenly place
Amen

July 9, 2023

Phyllis Comeaux

CHANGE OF HEART

Lord, here I sit wallowing in pride
But thinking of You, my thoughts go inside
Where I should think of Your love so true
And imitate You in all that I do
It's not about me and what I desire
But how to reach out and turn hearts afire
I beg You please, keep me on track
Harness selfish desires and give no slack
Expose my foolish errors every day
Show me how to correct them in Your way
Change my heart, O God

Let me see the inner beauty of souls
Beneath the pain, fear, anger or useless goals
And help me to pray for their change of heart
Have courage to stay with them and not depart
Or just love them and friend them along the way
And walk with them patiently every day
Give me your gentle caring demeanor
To massage their hearts until they surrender
And open up to Your love flowing freely
So we both want to be with You more dearly
You've changed our hearts, O God

You catch the tears as we fall to our knees
Thanking You for the gift of these little seeds
That You've planted and watered one by one

As we've walked along the path with the Son
Each little seed a sin that was buried deep below
Losing its seedcoat, exposing the embryo
Fertilized richly with Your everlasting love
Revealing what is hidden in the innermost chamber
That takes root in the depths of the fertilized soul
And cared for by You through your heavenly labor
We see the fruits that abound for days untold
A Change of Heart So Beautiful and Bold

July 19, 2023

MY BROKEN HEART

A heart that appears normal and strong
Can be broken in many ways
As the great physician examines what's wrong
He makes the incision that exposes all
Of the inner chambers and mechanisms
Finding clots that hinder the flow
Of the blood carrying love that helps me grow
The blood was tainted by outside forces
That slowly seeped in when I didn't know

While under the anesthesia of prayer
He asks directly "Do you want to be healed
Pondering the answer, do I ever dare
To respond "Yes, open me up for all to see"
So, He enters my heart body and all
Wearing His crown of thorns with dignity
And each pointy thorn pokes thru the lining
Which allows the bad blood to drip out
And the blood dripping from His head down His face
Begins the infusion that keeps me living

You must be still and stay in my care
From now until the end of your days
You will receive a booster in daily prayer
That will give you strength and grace
As your heart grows stronger, our love grows fonder
Which slows scarring and hastens the healing pace

So we never find ourselves apart
Come to me for your daily visit
To prevent anymore broken hearts

July 20, 2023

EACH AND EVERY DAY

I need you Jesus to come inside of me
Each and every day, but especially now
Settle my soul, end the battle
I am tired of hearing so much prattle
Coming at me from every direction
Trying to discern what needs correction
To give me peace and end the fight
That keeps me up day and night

Today, I'm being pulled in so many ways
It's hard to find time to give You praise
My thoughts are distracted, quickly fading away
Until I stop to contemplate You at end of day
Thank You for being there in my time of need
To calm my spirit and plant good seed
That will bear fruit unchoked by these weeds
Of distraction, irritation and aggravation

Stop and be quiet, empty your mind
Then open your heart, a welcoming sign
That you want Him near you until end of time
And mark you with His seal upon your soul
Forever and ever until you grow old
So you'll never be apart for days untold
Proclaiming His praises confident and bold

The days grow shorter as night comes in
I wonder if another day will begin
Now is the time to secure my place
Ask of Him an abundance of heavenly grace
So I can be with Him forevermore
To love Him and honor Him and always adore
The One who created me and loves me
Until time fades away and we are together
Each and every day

July 30, 2023

Phyllis Comeaux

LOVE DIVINE

You are the one who fills my heart
You are the one who nurtures my soul
You will always be with me until I grow old
And then stay near to me for days untold
As Your greatest desire and mine as well
Is to share our love to the depths of imagination
And then spread the fruit to the rest of creation
That they may know a love that burns in expectation
Never shrinking away in trepidation

You are the One who gives me life
And the One who takes away all strife
If I but open the door to let You in
So that our love affair will never end
Your knock is so soft, I sometimes don't hear
As I am distracted by things far and near
But knowing how often that this does happen
I resolve to be still until my senses heighten

Waiting for my bridegroom with my lamp
Keeping watch throughout the night
Memories of moments shared come to light
Giving me the patience to wait for the sound
That lets me know You are coming around
To scoop me in Your arms, take me away

That I may never fear harm another day
But remain with You until the end of time
Me and my Bridegroom in a Love Divine

September 12, 2023

HEAVEN AND EARTH KISS

Not a single kiss but many
Has He favored upon this world
Starting with all of creation
A love story slowly unfolds
As He breathed life into each creature
And painted the landscape with color
He looked around and said "It is Good"
Giving His kiss of approval

After the fall,
When they were banned from the Garden
Man and Woman began to roam the Earth
Adding to its numbers with every birth
But laden with sin as time went on
The Earth ceased to be a paradise
As quarrels, greed and selfishness
Reared its ugly head and God drew weary
Of the constant quarrels and obstinance
So He sent a Flood to wash them away
All but one Noah and his family
Lived to see another light of day

And on that day, came another kiss
As the gift from heaven filled the sky
With a beautiful bow of vibrant colors
Arched across the heavens way up high
To seal the promise that came from Heaven
Never another torrent would fall from the sky

To flood the Earth as in days gone by
But even so, man lost his way
Growing more distant from God each day

Then He dropped another kiss upon the Earth
As the virgin was blessed with a child
Who would save the world by His miraculous birth
The Son of God, so meek and so mild
Became the Savior who gave His very life
For the sake of the blessed and the wild
To end the inevitable damnation
On man and his stubborn abominations

The greatest act of love, the final kiss
A moment in time that is uniquely sublime
Evoking much emotion
In those with great devotion
Who witness the perpetual moment
When Heaven and Earth Kiss
As the priest holds up the Host
The BODY of CHRIST
And then the cup of wine
The BLOOD of CHRIST

And we open our lips to receive the kiss
That permeates through our body
Each and every time we receive the Eucharist
And fills our soul with longing and love
For the One sent from Heaven above
A kiss so deep that changes our hearts
And makes us one with Him never to part
The Final Kiss - Eternal Bliss
As Heaven and Earth Kiss

September 24, 2023

TREASURE CHEST

The Holy Spirit holds the key
To open the chest that holds the treasure
Which You have hidden just for me
To find one day, bringing much pleasure
I can't imagine what it will be
But I shall value it beyond measure

So Holy Spirit, I pray to thee
That you will never abandon me
But guide me daily, lead the way
On the journey every day
To find the gifts that you have hidden
Amongst your eloquent words of wisdom

Sitting so quiet, thoughts put aside
Your words come alive and speak to me
In visions, colors or ideas to contemplate
Which soon become cohesive and clear
So long as I am patient and wait
Anxious to find the treasure, I do not fear
But every morsel from you, I anticipate
I will cherish each bit and hold it so dear

As I gather these gifts each and every one
I put them in a very safe place
To have and to hold, to ponder upon
To unwrap one by one at a slow pace
A gem that is brilliant, shining its light
Illuminating words filled with grace
I keep in my chest always to treasure
Examining each one in my leisure

And each time I do, they seem to come anew
With a luster that beckons to me
Turning it in the light, there is a new hue
As you open my eyes to be able to see
The words of wisdom pouring from You
And a pearl of great price comes into view
And into my heart, my treasure chest

October 24, 2023

STORMY NIGHT

The storm this night is raging around
The wind blows with furious sounds
Spare me from all distraction Lord
So I may complete my tasks to do
That I may sit and ponder Your word
Letting me spend more time with You
And keep my mind upon those things
The Spirit deems as heavenly Truth
As He shelters me beneath His wings
So not to wander or grow aloof

Even with blinders my mind can wander
Though I try to change its course
To return to thee 'fore things go asunder
And I end up in a place much worse
I need to be in Your presence now
To fill my heart with love and peace
And keep me in thy tender care
Protect me from unworldly beasts
That prowl about while I'm unaware
Tripping me up, like slipping in grease
Causing a fall that is truly unfair

 Vulnerable I sit with open heart
Closing my eyes to all distraction
Praying for your grace to give me the start
To remove from my mind all infractions

That can form a wedge which pull us apart
Quiet, be still, silence is golden
To You only am I beholden
Nothing will ever come between us
If I can help it, without fail, I must
This I know, ever in Your will, I trust

The storm has settled; the wind, a whisper
My heart is still, my mind is quiet
All is calm as in the dark of night
One by one stars begin to appear
And wishes with hope erase my fear
For I know for sure that You are near
And together our Love grows so dear
As we sit in the dark counting stars
And blessings fall upon all whom you love
Like showers of grace from heaven above
Good Night, I love You

November 3, 2023

WELCOME HOME

Slowly sails the ship into the harbor
A safe haven, to recover at last
Battered and torn, the sails on the mast
Weathered and beaten with holes in the hull
The tired vessel makes its way to the dock
With a lopsided movement toward us all
As one with a peg leg who lilts to one side
It finds its way home with no sense of pride
The battle was won but the cost was so dear
As some lives were lost, all shed a tear

From where comes this ship? Ask the hands on the dock
Sailing the seas looking for true treasures?
Or searching the lands for worldly pleasures?
Getting distracted as they stopped to play
They found themselves lost along the way
Trying to find the way back home
They found themselves caught up in a storm
Tossed hither and yonder and turned around
'Til they heard the call home, heeding the sound

Thus, the wayward Christian finds a way home
After darting off without a look back
Going after distractions that got him off track
Content and enjoying himself for a while
He finds he is missing home in this trial
And turns to see no one to help find the way

So he drops to his knees to fervently pray
And in the dark and stillness of night
He hears the call that changes his plight
Come Home to me and I will hold you tight
FOREVER – was the word that set him right

December 9, 2023
(on retreat)

COME HOLY SPIRIT

Come, Holy Spirit
Enter my heart
To order my day
From the very start
As I kneel to pray
Fill me with much love
That I may give some away
To those most in need
Throughout this blessed day

Also, dear Spirit
I regret to say
There are things in my heart
That should not stay
Judging others is not right
Lest they judge me, what a fright
Selfishness, another one
Sharing gifts is much more fun

Distractions come
Throughout the day
At Mass, or work
Or when I pray
I need you now
To stop the flow
Of all these thoughts
That just must go

So fill me now
To the brim
That I may focus
Just on Him
The one that I
So much adore
And want to be with
Forevermore

December 10, 2023
(on retreat)

INTO THE DEPTHS OF MY SOUL

Mother Mary, Holy Spirit
Come into my Soul
Guide me thru this treacherous world
Protect me from evil swirling about
And ward off all dangers as they unfurl
Be my sensor to emit a warning
That I may know when I stray from the path
Chasing butterflies that flit all around
And are so alluring without a sound
Then out of my sight, I collapse with a frown

A useless chase, a waste of time
What did I expect to gain all the while
Then I look about to see where I've gone
And feel I am lost as though in exile
How could I have strayed so far from home
When all I wanted was a little pleasure
I must find the way back, sure not to roam
Where is the sign that shows me the way
I cannot believe how far I have gone
Look up to Mary and the Spirit to pray

His Mother has heard me calling her name
As she listens for the sound of my voice
Then heeds the prayer and sends the Spirit

To guide me back on the Way I should be
And He doesn't ever leave my side
'Til he's sure my roaming days are done
And even then, He stays so close to me
I know that I will always be safe, yet free
So I quickly fall down upon my knees
Offering praise and thanks for taking care of me
Coming down into the depths of my soul

December 16, 2023

ON THIS QUIET MORN

Born a wee baby
So tiny and small
You came down to earth
To be Savior of all

Mary, your mother
Filled with Spirit and grace
Said Yes to the angel
And the whole human race

With stars in the sky
On a midnight clear
The Heavens were filled
As angels appeared
Lighting the night
With glorious cheer

As songs from above
Reached those tending sheep
In the depths of the night
Touched their hearts so deep

Go to the stable
Where the babe is asleep
Amongst animals and doves
Find a sign of true love

Gazing upon Him
His parents in awe
A miracle of life
Lying in the straw

Peace and wonder all around
As shepherds and creatures
Bowed to the ground
A Savior was born
And Him we have found
On this quiet morn

December 28, 2023

NEVER TOO LATE

Through the window of my room
As I gaze into the night
To wish upon a star
I pray with all my might
That You hear me from afar
Trepidation in my plight
Has given me quite a jar

Keeping time spent with You
Has often eluded me
Though I know Your love is true
I sometimes fail to see
What's shrouded in my view
As I focus on the tree
That has the golden fruit

Here I lie in this bed
My fate unknown for now
Thoughts are swirling in my head
To put You first, I should vow
To turn to You instead
Of going off away from thou
Searching pleasures, I should dread

"Not too late to come to Me"
I hear so loud and clear
"Ever watching over thee
You have no need to fear
As the love you pour on others
I see and find so dear
And so I pour my love on you
Hoping to draw you near"

January 6, 2024

I HEAR YOUR CALL

I hear Your call, O Lord
It stirs in my heart
As I ponder Your word
Prodding me to start
Slashing with a sword
That which keeps me apart
As though tethered by a cord
Which makes me come up short
Never moving forward

It's time to move ahead
And take an active part
There's no reason to dread
The Spirit moves your heart
And then stirs in your head
Plans and passion to start
Reaching out to spread
What life is all about

"Please," I ask, "cut the cord"
And let me not fear
Knowing You're true to your word
And will always be near
So that I can let go
To share the Good News
And do as You ask
No need to be blue
What's holding me back

I'm ashamed to say
That I have great fear
That overshadows the way
Draining any confidence
Interrupting as I pray
Letting distractions come in
Whatever am I to say
Please free me from myself
So I can begin, if I may

"Let go and do what I do
Love and be loved
By all who come to you
Travel hither and fro
To complete the task
Sharing the Good News
Without agenda or mask
Hear the sound of my call
As I hold you in my palm
You will never fall"

January 8, 2024

WILD RIDE

Like a wild horse
Untethered and free
I run like the wind
Throughout the country
I have not the mind
Nor the will to sit still
As moving and running
Are what give me a thrill

But where am I going
Is the question at hand
Am I running away
Or going on a search?
I do not know this day
For if I stop, what then?
I may get lost, lose my way
Finding myself at a dead end

Do you hear what you say?
Keep running to no end
Might be wise to stop and pray
For a sign on where to begin
And start on a journey today
The Spirit of God, much like the wind
Moves swiftly, giving a thrill
To those open to His will

Although the freedom of the run
In the wild that seems to be such fun
Is often the start of the end
As I sense growing discontent
So, I should stop and take a rest
Sensing this Spirit knows what's best
Clear my head and look around
Open my heart to what I've found

Now is the time as the day has begun
With clouds in the sky glowing in sun
As warmth and peace wash over me
Knowing I won't long be locked in a pen
I must be still and wait, don't give in
To those feelings of discontent
And the gate flies open, I am free
The journey ends in love and peace
With the Spirit watching over me

January 14, 2024

Phyllis Comeaux

THE JOY OF SUFFERING

The joy of suffering
A paradox for sure
As just the thought of pain
So difficult to endure
How did our Lord refrain
From the urge to pass the cup
As He sweat drops of blood
When His time was about up

Yet persevere He did
To restore the fate of man
Who marred the beauty given
By falling prey to sin
Leading to life with suffering
Upsetting the plan of God
Our Jesus took it on Himself
So our peace could be restored

A love so great, He gave His life
Enduring much pain and strife
We cannot even begin
To know what it was like
Much less to imagine a joy
That He held so deep inside
In spite of every lash and strike
That tore His body apart
To atone for all the sin
That man himself did start

46

The joy He found in suffering and pain
Was all for our final destiny
That we could ever be with Him again
And the Father for all eternity
So we must follow in His footsteps
And look for the joy that goes with pain
There is a plan for our suffering
And if we unite it with the cross
We can find joy deep inside
That we have eased some of the pain
That our Lord endured way back then
Amen

January 16, 2024

THE BANQUET

Come and share in the banquet
Prepared by His mighty hand
Never has been such eloquence
The finest in all the land
Heed his call, ready yourself
A spread of such abundance
Some bites sweet, others nourish
All are meant to share
But don't be late, dress with flourish
The Host prefers those who prepare

Step into the gathering Hall
Your name He will proudly call
For He has seen the deeds you do
And knows the depths of your heart
As you have pondered His word
And acted on what you've heard
You have received Him nearly every day
And taken the time to be fed and pray
You have shared Him with others
And fed them as well
With sweetness and love abounding

Come to my table, Eat with me
For you I have prepared this feast
You are my precious favored one
Definitely not one of the least

As I look about at those all around
I feel like I am bare and naked
For they are aglow, unaware of it though
As I see them adorned with a halo
I want to turn and quickly go
For surely this mistake is unknown

Then in the corners, huddled together
I spy a group that seems quite frightened
Some faces I know from long ago
And the years have not lightened
The burdens they continue to carry
But here in this place, they will find a face
That welcomes them to the banquet
For under their garments, shining so bright
Is the love and kindness, faith and light
That helped them persist in their plight

The music begins and I am taken in
By the sound of the harps and the lyres
Before I know it the dancing begins
And I know I'll be staying to the end
I'm floating on the floor quite unaware
Drawing others to come and share
The grace flowing all around and about
Then out of my mouth comes such a shout
"Come all who are hungry and weary"
For the Lord knows all you've been through
And He's hosting this party for you

January 18, 2024

Phyllis Comeaux

IN THE SHADOW OF YOUR WINGS

I hope I will always be
In the shadow of your wings
As you hover and protect me
From all worldly harmful things
For I have sought you without fail
And spent much time with you
Wondering if 'twas to no avail
At times, has made me kind of blue

Then suddenly I realize
You have been there all along
I couldn't see you with my eyes
Because you had me under your wing
So I thought I was in total darkness
Afraid, alone, no reason to sing
Then You pull me out into the light
And suddenly, I see everything

My shelter in the shadow of your wings
Has made me bold and daring
And I go forth, Your praises to sing
Reaching out to all, Your true love I'm sharing
Filled with Your Spirit while under your wing
I can soar with His grace to heights far above
Swooping down to touch those who seem blue
Drawing close and sharing Your love so true
As You have done for me and others too

And when I am tired or the day is all done
I find myself restless for the time to go home
Back to my shelter under your wings
As I know there, I am never alone
I can relax and let go of my fears
If needed, let loose a torrent of tears
Feel the comfort and safety of this shelter
That I find nearby in the Shadow of your wings

February 8, 2024

LOVE, PEACE AND GLORY

In the peace of Your love
Your glory surrounds it all
And slowly they meld together
Love, Peace and Glory
Settling deep into my soul
No longer anxious and hungry
Begging for a morsel of You
Leaving me content and filled
For I have received a good portion
That will carry me all this day through

As I go out to the World
After rising from prayer
Full to the brim, eager to share
This love and peace that overflows
Searches for those needing some care
Even though they may be unaware
Aiming at their heart piercing so deep
With a transfusion of love and peace
That slowly surrounds them with glory
Drawing them deep into this story

And they are transformed as I once was
Filled yet hungry for even more
As my palate has tasted immense pleasure
Traveling through all my senses
They too are aware of this treasure

As they go about their business
Sharing it in all their endeavors
With those intrigued by their wisdom
And drawn in by their demeanor

So the circle spreads like a ripple
From a single stone in the water
Cast out with a toss so simple
Yet traveling shore to shore
A circle that has no bounds
Continuing to reach out all around
Adding to this perpetual story
Of sharing your Love, Peace and Glory

February 10, 2024

BURNING DESIRE

Come into the depths of my heart today
To stir up the ashes that lie within
Barely smoldering, dormant in disarray
Set ablaze a fire to burn away sin
The cause of the angst and dismay
That plagues my soul now and again
But give me a burning desire this day
To replace it with love for You and all men

The Holy Spirit hovering about
Takes heed to my call and moves on in
His wings spread wide, He stirs the ashes
Igniting a flame that begins to burn
Disintegrating the sin that lurks within
Exposing the places prone to return
To the distasteful habits of my sin
Over and over, they tend to repeat
Making me weary and succumb to defeat

Like a grinding stone or planer
He scrapes and smooths the surface
Removing hiding places in the cracks
Not without pain or grief
But bear it, I must, until it's revived
Filling the gaps with love and grace

So that all sin is gone without a trace
And the process repeats over and over
Until all is smooth with nowhere to hide
And I am worthy to be by His side

And day by day, one by one
I draw closer to Father and Son
Without the distraction of rubbish and sin
That has plagued me often deep within
Now supplanted with a burning desire
To stay close to You forevermore
And remain with You in a Love lit by fire

February 11, 2024

FRUITS OF THE HOLY SPIRIT

Tongues of Fire
leap into my heart
Burn away the rubbish
And all the disgrace
That has crept into
Your lovely dwelling place

Wings of the dove
Fly into my Soul
Sweeping up the ash
Making room for love
Settle into me
With Your heavenly peace

Breath of Wind
Whisper in my Ear
The words of the Song
You wish me to hear
To guide my day
And keep me near

Cloud of Glory
Surround me with protection
And envelope me forever
Leading me in the right direction
Heading to the Promised land
Revealing Your presence
As You take me by the hand

Waters of Life
Pour over me, into me, immerse me
Wash away all iniquity
Raise me up again
Free and clean from the stain of sin
Quench the overwhelming thirst
As I experience the sacrament of rebirth

Bread of Heaven
As the Spirit hovers over the altar
The bread of Heaven is transformed
Into the Body of Christ
Our spiritual nourishment
Feeding our souls every day
Changing our hearts to be like Yours

Drink of Salvation
Along with the bread, we are able to drink
The cup of salvation
As the wine becomes the blood
That was shed on the day
of the death of our Lord
To give us New Life

Through the prayers of the faithful
We remember Him and thank Him for these gifts
That bring us new and everlasting life
Just as His death opened the gates of Heaven
And His resurrected body was taken up
To sit on the throne next to His Father
Calling each of us home to be forever with Him

February 12, 2024

GIFTS FROM GOD

God sends us the rain
So we appreciate the Sun
And never take in vain
All the wonders He has done
And then to top it off
He adorns it with a bow
Of many vibrant colors
That makes quite a show

Likewise, He sends His only Son
To live and walk with us
A light to all the world
Much like the yellow sun
Though He shines even at night
Even in darkness nailed to the cross
The light is present for all to see
That His is the Way it must be

Another heavenly treasure
His Mother Mary lights the Way
And teaches us all how to pray
And say yes to God with such grace
In spite of alarm and dismay
In a fashion no mother could face
But follow her footsteps today
That much sorrow you can embrace
Should it ever come your way

No other treasure is like the Spirit
That comes to us in so many ways
In the whisper of the breeze or
Howling wind through the trees
A light touch upon my soul or
Filling me full from head to toe
A dose of wisdom He can bestow
Or give me a push on the edge of a peak
That I must trust Him as I leap

So many gifts come my way
Adorned by grace, wrapped in love
And so much more when I pray
Showered with peace from above
I do not deserve such love and kindness
But I am so thankful for His goodness
And He calls me to come and be near
As He whispers in my ear
"You are mine"
A gift

February 13, 2024

MOTHER MARY, HOLY SPIRIT

Come into my Soul
Guide me thru this treacherous world
Protect me from the evil swirling about
And ward off all dangers as they unfurl
Be my sensor to emit a warning
That I may know when I stray from the path
Chasing butterflies that flit all around
Causing me to trip and fall on my face
Making me realize I've been a disgrace

Holy Spirit, center me then set me free
With wings of a dove, I glide over the sea
Glancing around with keen eyes like an eagle
You lead me to the places where there is a need
In so many others who want to be freed
Swooping down below, I tip them with my wing
So you can pour out your love, lift them up high
Without another prompt, they begin to sing
And soon they will join me soaring the skies
Singing your praises that float down to the Earth
Thanking our God for the chance of rebirth

Our Mother Mary looks on with approval
As the children of God are celebrating
The gifts that have poured down on them

By the grace of the Spirit that is within
As Mary has prompted this global happening
My prayer has been answered this day
and touched many more to pray
For grace to stay on the path
And never again to stray
Reside within our souls each day
Mother Mary, Holy Spirit

February 25, 2024

HOPE—A NEW DAWN

In the dark night when the soul seems lost
There seems so little chance to be found
Never really finding the way
As we meander all around
The door seems closed as we try to pray
Our thoughts in silence peal like a gong
Ringing in our ears a distracting sound
Cover your ears, hide your eyes
Nowhere to turn for reprise

Center yourself, draw yourself in
No, open your heart and just be still
Listen for the voice within
My ears may be deaf, I cannot hear
Only the darkness is steady, I fear
Will there be hope to see the light
To hear the sounds that calm the fright
Be still, again, and wait for me
And soon you will be able to see
Even in darkness, I am there
So, be patient and don't despair

Slowly I start to feel a glow
That may even give me hope
Coming with a glimmer of light?

Decreasing the darkness of night
Could this be the start of dawn
That I may see the light of the morn
Hearing the sounds of the new day
Giving me incentive to pray
Pouring out love and emotion for the gift
That gives me hope as it uplifts
Never taking for granted again
The Hope of a New Dawn within

February 25, 2024

Phyllis Comeaux

ANOINTED PRIEST, PROPHET AND KING

Each of us at our Baptism
Born into the Family of God
As waters of Life poured over us
Giving us all reasons to sing
Praise and thanksgiving for this gift
As He calls us all to so many things
That teach us to serve and uplift
Those sent to us on angel's wings

Our priestly role imitates Christ
During the Holy Sacrifice of Mass
As we offer ourselves up to God
A personal outpouring of love and sacrifice
Along with our gifts in communion
With the bread and the wine
That the Priest offers up on our behalf
In thanksgiving for His love divine
And the promise of eternal life

As prophets, we proclaim the gospel
By the way we live and speak the truth
According to the Word of the Lord
We are the Church that goes out to serve
Bringing Jesus to all that we meet
Reaching out to all those in need

Filling the void that helps them to see
The One who loves to give life
To all those living in strife

As varied as our "Kingdoms", our Kingly roles
Look different according to our lives
Nevertheless, we must take charge
And live up to the promises we made
Reaching out to all the subjects
Who live and play within our boundary
Directing them towards the truth
Setting them straight on the path
To fulfill them as priest, prophet and king
That leads to a share of eternal life in
The Heavenly Kingdom that is our destiny
As we live out these roles into eternity

February 25, 2024

SURRENDER

What is it to surrender?
To some it means to lose freedom
Or be taken captive unwillingly
Maybe never to see the light of day
Or run about with others to play
Nor be able to worship and pray
In this case, it's a very sad day
Forced on those stalked as prey
Bound and loathed, pushed to a corner
Left to die, sad and dishonored

Sometimes surrender can lead to freedom
For those who choose to rid themselves
Of that which leads to darkness within
As they offer their souls to be purged
Of all that has a hold on their heart
Blinding them from seeing their sin
Until the day they are chagrined
Willingly throwing themselves to the fire
To burnish loathsome habits and desires

The ash is left, unrecognizable as sin
Weeping often is part of the process
As the soul parts from the desires of flesh
But the relief that follows is like a spring rain
That brings new growth and a full life again
Coming out of darkness into the sun
Where the light leads them to the Holy one
Who will accompany them the rest of the way
As they invite Him into their soul every day

March 5, 2024

PIT OF SACRIFICE

With Lent comes the chance to sacrifice
As we follow in the steps of our Lord
Giving up what distracts us from Him
Throwing the rocks we stumble on into the pit
As well as the weeds and brambles
That get under our skin, irritating and annoying
Making us stop and search around
For that which has altered our course
From the one that we intended to be on
A smooth and steady road leading to salvation

How did we wander onto this rocky path
Are we so distracted to have become lost
Then in one aberrant step we fall into the pit
And we fervently pray for a bit of sight
As we frantically try to scramble to the top
But to no avail, as there is no way
To scale the walls to see the light of day
And we crumple to the floor in such dismay
But in the distance, we discern a voice
From where it comes, I cannot say

And intently, we strain to hear the word
Almost certain that it comes from Jesus, our Lord
This is not a trap He says with compassion
As you're experiencing what I did in my Passion
Stumbling and falling on the Way to the Cross

Sweating with anticipation of what comes next
Moving forward toward the darkness
Knowing for certain, there is no other way
To bring about salvation for one and all
Which is why you too have heeded the call

He seems to draw close to offer a choice
You may move forward on this Way of the Cross
That is meant to save souls who are lost
You will continue to stumble and fall
But I will offer my hand, help carry you
When you are so worn and tired
Heading towards the light far above the pit
And on the last steps I will give the final lift
That raises you up as I did on the third day
So that out of the pit of sacrifice
You will be with me in Eternal Life

March 9, 2024

THE COCOON

There was a day when I was born anew
Bursting out of my cocoon
Coming into the light from the darkness
Shriveled and stuck in my old form
That was lowly and resembled a worm
But now as I breathed in new life
My wings began to expand
And unfurl the amazing array of
Colors that emerged in the light of day
Breathtakingly beautiful they say

The light is so bright
The sun is so warm
And I am filled with delight
Throughout the world, I begin to roam
Into the heavens and out of sight
Not having a place to call home
But I am not at all filled with fright
As God is with me wherever I go
As I flit around to and fro
Finding a haven in a place dimly lit
As I curl up on a branch of respite

As the morning light emerges
My wings unfold in a radiant display
As a breath of you within me surges
To help guide me along the way

As I begin to soar through the sky
To find the ones who faithfully prayed
That you would send a gift from on high
To help them all through their dismay
So they can emerge from the dark of night
Into the brilliance of the new day
Finding much joy as they find the Light
That will guide them forever on their Way
Once out of The Cocoon

March 10, 2024

DIVINE MOMENTS

I look far up to the Heavens
With my hands raised to the sky
That You may lift me out of this place
And take me to the promise on high
Away from this torment and disgrace
Approaching You, I let out a sigh
Leaving all behind without a trace
For Your comfort and peace, I draw nigh
Never to lose sight of your face

Your loving eyes pierce into my soul
Drawing me close from the inside out
You touch those parts that I should hold
As Your treasures to me from of old
That I may cherish in times of stress
And ease the symptoms of duress
How can I forget these special moments
When I have soared high to the summit
Upon Your wings with heavenly grace
Returning at the end of my prayer
To find that I am still in my chair

Wait, don't leave I want You to stay
But knowing there will be another day
Another time for us to be close
So being recharged with Your gift of love
As you continue to shower it from above

Mirrors of Faith

I wonder why I gave into despair
For I truly know You are always there
Even when I can't feel Your presence
I can hold onto the essence
Of the memory and moment divine
Knowing You will always be mine

March 11, 2024

MIRROR OF FAITH

As I come to You
I quiet my soul
That you may come inside
And search for the beauty within
That which you have created
For I seem to have lost it
Feeling ugly and barren
Asking why and where it is hidden

You pull out a mirror
And hand it over to me
As you patiently explain
"The beauty of a soul, my child
Is found in Humility
That comes from within
But cannot be seen
'Til you work to remove pride
That hides deep inside"

Pride comes of what I want to be
And work to make sure others see
That blemished part of me
That is not really true
So they never find what God sees
When He looks into my soul
A flower of sweetness and beauty
With petals of love, peace, compassion
Upon a strong stem of Humility
That is being hidden from humanity

"Having a mirror of Faith
Will allow you to see
The image that I
Have created for thee
One of sweetness and love
Adorned with purity
You are doing your best
Trying so hard to please me"

"Look again at the reflection
And gaze deeply within
You will see a heart of LOVE
That emanates from the mirror like an echo
A message that does not quiver with fear
But strong solid unwavering
With the TRUST you have in your soul
No matter what comes your way
Faith is with you every day"

Finally, as I gaze away
I find I am left with an aura
Of pure joy and peace
As we have met in the Mirror
I remain still and quiet
Contemplating the image
That has moved me deep inside
And filled me with love and grace
To see the beauty of my soul
In the Mirror of Faith

February 27, 2024

Phyllis Comeaux

PERSONAL POEMS FOR MY FAMILY

Here the author presents poems for members of the family. Each person was presented with a copy of the poem.

Phyllis Comeaux

A VERY SPECIAL BIRTHDAY

This is the day that the Lord hath made
And on this day, a baby boy was born
To a fine couple who loved him so
While they taught, nurtured and watched him grow
Curly haired tot with an inviting smile
Who loves baseball, golf, and music
Reading, history and learning new things
Throughout his "Berry" town upbringing
Leading to a future beyond his dreams

Forty years later, into a man he's grown
One of the finest that we have known
Gentle and quiet is his demeanor
Taking seriously his every endeavor
Including a young maiden named Julie
Who piqued his interest Trulie
With her witty banter in correspondence
That eventually led to the first date
And the rest of the story is fate

God has blessed this union Trulie
With not one, but three precious boys
Multiplying love exponentially
With each unique personality
That was born of the love of the two

Filling their days in so many ways
As the head of the family he prays
And teaches them all to give glory
To the God who unfolded this story
On this day that the Lord hath made

November 24, 2023
(For Trevor's birthday)

Phyllis Comeaux

TRUE LOVE

True love has its destiny
And finds the one meant for eternity
For some, they must be patient and wait
'Til they find the one meant to be their mate
But on the day, God is present and graces flow
And it doesn't take long for them to know
Their lives are meant to be joined together
United as one, now through forever

The happy day is like a fairy tale
And everyone present wishes them well
But in Heaven above is the real celebration
As God made the plan on the day of creation
And the angels were present as they held hands
Singing their praise as they exchanged bands
A sign of the union that would last a lifetime
Shrouded in love that encompasses the divine

From that love and union, a family grew
And each time their love also multiplies
For the one that is precious and new
Welcomed and cherished with love in their eyes
The family together strengthen their ties
One to the other and to God up above
As Jesus and the Spirit teach them to love
Those in their care and all around
As they are all called to be Heaven bound

The story continues to eternity
As we all know this is our destiny
We all help each other along the way
And the Spirit is present every day
With wisdom we turn to Him and humbly pray
For guidance and blessings in every endeavor
And the grace to be with Him and each other forever

November 12, 2023
(For Julie and Trevor's anniversary)

PALMER

Palmer, my grandson, my sweet little one
Dreaming of you as bright as the sun
Filling the room with coos and gurgles
Smiling, laughing, making bubbles
Who will you be like, I wonder
One that fills a room with thunder
Or meek, mild like a little lamb
Swaddled so cozy in your pram

Loving and loved you will certainly be
Surrounded by family waiting to see
Your precious little hands and tiny face
Fashioned by God and sprinkled with grace
Your brothers will teach you many things
To play and climb and learn to swing
Your parents will give an abundance of love
Matched only by that from Heaven above

Praying for you always my little one
To grow healthy and strong under the sun
To love the Lord, God with all your heart
As He has been with you from the start
Blessing your family with the great news
That another Lemaire would join the crew
And all of your cousins waiting for you
To add to the chaos of the family zoo
We Love You

October 15, 2023
(2 days prebirth)

PALMER JOSEPH

Sweet baby boy, seventh grandchild
From his first days, greets me with a smile
Eyes wide and bright, laughter within
Soon starts to coo and draw you in
He holds your gaze while kicking his feet
Full of energy as our eyes meet
And so much joy erupts in his chair
He might jump into my arms from there
Except that he's just two months old
Already with a story to be told

Another great feat is raising his head
While on his tummy in his bed
All babies do that you might say
But not all on the very first day
I can already tell he loves to play
And we will have fun in many ways
Just as he will with his big brothers
Emmitt James and Meyer John
Who've loved and adored him from day one

So gentle and sincere were the first words
At the first glance into the bassinet
"I love you, Palmer"
As he reached in to touch him ever so soft
And that scene is ingrained in my mind
It brought tears to my eyes, melted my heart

To witness such gentleness and love
I knew they are off to a good start
With wonderful parents and God's grace
To hold them all in a heavenly embrace

February 25, 2024

MEYER
Age 3

Precious little boy
With a curly topped head
Beaming from ear to ear
As he bursts through the door
To give a big hug and get a kiss
While I squeeze him, holding him tight
A moment I don't want to miss
Eyes sparkling with delight
He melts my heart to the core

He looks at me with stars in his eyes
Whispering 'I love you Mimi' so quiet
And I pick him up and hold him high
And I whisper "I love you too"
He rests his head on my shoulder
And I wish he'd never grow older
But Heaven knows, He will surely grow
And I will soon have to let him go

But for now, it is such a great pleasure
To hold and cuddle, feed and love him
Giving thanks for the blessing and treasure
For in a moment, he will run off in a whim
When the last of the oatmeal is scooped
I watch him scamper with an impish grin

And letting out a boyish whoop
Got things to do like building with blocks
Or playing with trains that go "choo choo"

Fill in the gaps with moments of quiet
Reading books is one of his delights
Never one to pass up a hug
Or cuddle on the sofa like a love bug
He makes my day in so many ways
There is much to offer up in praise
As we spend the whole day together
Creating more memories each day

July 8, 2023

AUTUMN

Our special girl, Autumn, is turning four
A perfect age to start to explore
The world around her and so much more
Like her favorite explorer whom she adores
Who also solves mysteries and wears a crown
But never on her face will you see a frown
Because she is smart, strong and confident
And will persevere 'til she finds evidence

The world is wide open to you our sweet girl
To learn an abundance and try your hand
At all the possibilities found in the land
You've already tried so many things to this day
And you're good at so many, if I must say
Like dancing, learning and playing sports
And imagining, building creations of all sorts
It's a delight and privilege to watch you grow
And blossom like a flower ready to bloom

Wait! She's dashing away to another room
Catch her if you can, but you will have to zoom
As her feet fly through the air and scamper away
Before you can blink an eye, then turn to play
The only clue for you is the giggle you hear
Somewhere out there, but is she near
Quick, don't delay, get up and go play
She is going to grow up and then we will say

Where is Autumn?
Out and about with friends today

I'm so very happy to have this time now
To laugh, pretend and frolic about
I treasure each moment as a gift from above
And thank the Lord God for this one to love
While I pray for her always as she grows
That you keep her safe as Heaven knows
The world about needs so much of your grace
To cover the path as she goes place to place
Take care of her Lord, My Autumn Renee

November 11, 2023

MY SISTER

My Sister, my friend
A bond deep within
As long as I can remember
Since her birth in September
We've always been close
Sharing untold secrets
That only our hearts and blinking eyes
Revealed the truths held in disguise

Hours of fun, imagination in play
Such as school and restaurant
And come what may
Like hopscotch and jumprope
Then baby dolls to Barbie dolls
Or Animal Talk and Green Ghost
Laughing so silly or scared as could be
Charades, seances another kind of fun
Enjoyed by family, friends, everyone

What did you say?!
Tata dahling, this is the way
To lift your pinkie as you sip your tea
And pass the canapé on to me
Being grownup was fun to play
And makes me smile to this very day
Though being a child has slipped away
There's loads of fun in our grownup days

As we sip our wine with charcuterie
And plan a menu as elegant could be
Then shopping and nails, wine tasting galore
Being together, what we treasure more
Than any present that comes from a store
Sitting and talking, sharing and giving
I love her now and forevermore
She is my sister, my friend

♥

September 26, 2023

Phyllis Comeaux

MY BROTHER

One of a kind, all would agree
Confident in every degree
Growing up with sisters, makes three
Middle child he preferred not to be
But such was fate, so he took the lead
At times bold, unbridled and daring
Concocting explosives in the utility
Scraping by with a good scaring
Challenging all to establish his place
Making it to the top without disgrace

Often compassionate and caring
Endearing others in his kindness
Charming them in genuine acts of goodwill
He has an abundance of close friends
That love and care for him as we all do
As he has many ways of drawing us close
And we are so honored for him as our host
As he prepares gourmet meals fit for a king
Treats us to fine wine, bourbon or so many things
Teaches us games that we all love to play
And takes us around to new sites each day

Master of dinner parties, King of the Grill
The ones getting invited are always quite thrilled
Seven course meals are often the fare
And the menu leaves nothing to spare

The table is set as for a fine banquet
Silverware in its place for every course
Wine glasses appropriate for each pairing
The menu on a pedestal as you enter the room
And a cocktail or aperitif is offered soon

How did MY brother come to do all of this
By experiencing much in his life
And trying it out for himself
We are so grateful to be guinea pigs
And learn the art of fine dining
Plus all the other fun things we adore
My Brother, the doctor, computer nerd, entrepreneur,
master chef, golfer, fisherman, card shark…..
But always, my Brother

March 3, 2024

Phyllis Comeaux

MY TRUE LOVE

He is my one true love
The one sent to me from Heaven above
As our eyes met from across the room
While the music played and couples danced
We smiled from a distance as if by chance
Never dreaming 'twas the beginning of romance

He had played the piano for the show
That I had danced to on the stage
With all the girls in Angel Flight
As we entertained the ROTC that night
After the show, it was fate
That he had no date
And mine was going to be late

Standing by the bar so nonchalant
Beckoning beautiful blue eyes
His was such a genuine smile
I dare not approach for I was so shy
But he certainly did catch my eye
And strolled on over to say Hi

We shared about our current life
Again, the band began to play
No more talking let's just dance
And so we did for just a bit
Until my Navy boyfriend strolled on in
Picked me up at the waist
And carried me off as his date

No one could ever say
That was the end that day
Because John did search high and low
To find the girl who danced in the show
Who piqued his interest in a short time
Asking around, not waiting perchance
That she would turn up like a fairytale romance
So that he was determined he would find
This girl that he couldn't get out of his mind

And lo and behold it twas fate
That they finally had a very first "date'
Going to the park to play on the swings
And talking on about so many things
A more formal date was soon arranged
At Toby's Oak Grove, with music and wine
A very nice meal and amazing conversation
With this eloquent young man of many talents
Whom I would not be ashamed to meet my parents

So you can guess the end, I am sure my friend
As we have never parted to this very day
Except for a brief time that gave us a chance
To know this was not a short romance
But a lifetime with a future that we could not write
But God in His wisdom would make it all right
As we courted and broke up and got back together
This time knowing we were in it forever
And the rest is history with my true love
As God smiles on from Heaven above

March 11, 2024

ACKNOWLEDGEMENTS

I would like to thank all of those who have helped to inspire this second volume of poetry along with the Holy Spirit, as many of the poems have evolved from praying about or for specific people and their circumstances. I will not name them all, but they (or you) may recognize themselves or situations in some of these poems. Most of it, however, comes from my own experiences as well.

Obviously, I must again acknowledge the St Joseph Abbey Retreat Center and the powerful encounters with the Spirit that I have had there. You can see by the photo on the cover how beautiful and peaceful it is. Once you cross over the bridge onto the Abbey grounds, it's like being transported to another world. All of the retreat Directors, the Archbishop, monks, priests and support staff who have made my annual retreat since 2010 a very rich and growth filled experience. And I continue to be inspired on the Abbey grounds with one or more poems, as the setting and silence allow me to hear the still small voice of the Spirit. My special retreat friends Faye, Maddie, and Rachel have shared this journey with me every year as we travel there together. Faye also helped me decide on the cover photo which captures the mirror effect and the faith symbols beautifully.

I would also like to acknowledge the ACTS retreats and prayer groups that I have been involved in since my first retreat in 2016. Once again, teaming the Spring retreat in 2023, the Spirit continued to inspire several poems during that time.

As I mentioned before, Ashton Mouton, continues to encourage and inspire me. He put me in touch with Mr John Robb, who is involved with Welcome Home Catholics in Memphis, just as I was discerning to revive this Ministry in Lafayette after the pause we took during the pandemic.

We will be hosting a workshop this April (2024) for parishes to learn how to promote this movement. This was the inspiration for the poem Welcome Home that was written at the Abbey on the last morning of retreat.

Once again, I would like to acknowledge my most enthusiastic supporter, John, who continues to patiently read and offer suggestions or edits on some of the poems and graciously lets me know when it's "perfect as is" and must have "heard the Spirit" with perfect hearing.

He is my role model to perfect all of my writing and gently insists on improvements once in a while, which I do value. And I thank him for his encouragement, his patience and time in helping this come together for my family and friends and growing circle of outreach. John is the book designer, cover designer, editor, and publisher.

ABOUT THE AUTHOR

Born and raised in South Louisiana, and a life-long Roman Catholic, Phyllis constantly seeks a closer relationship with her Lord. She is committed to her Spiritual formation and growing deeper in the love and service that stem from the fruits of her daily Mass, prayer time and adoration. She is thankful to her parents, grandparents, Godparents as true examples of trust and faith in God and their unwavering commitment to being faithful in prayer and practicing their Catholic faith.

She is also thankful for the many ongoing spiritual growth and formation opportunities including ACTS, Bible Studies, podcasts, two very special prayer groups- the "Monday group" and the "Grimes group" in which I am the "middle child" – older than the younger group and younger than the older group, but both very special to me. While on St Joseph Abbey retreats with mostly the same group known as the M&M group (standing for motherhood and menopause) for the past 14 years and counting and various other retreats I have often received inspiration for some of these poems.

And finally the experience of a Catholic cruise with a huge company of married catholic couples and 16 priests including Fr. Mike Schmitz on the Good News Cruise. So the adventures and the journey continue with much fervor and excitement around every corner. Still with the final passage in view, the last voyage on the journey that will take me to meet my Bridegroom who hands me a Mirror of Faith, that I may see the beauty of the soul that was open to receive what He has shaped in my prayer time and beyond.

www.ingramcontent.com/pod-product-compliance
Lightning Source LLC
Chambersburg PA
CBHW031325040426
42443CB00005B/218